# CONTENTS

The Waiting Line

Copyright

INTRODUCTION                                    1

WHAT NOT TO SAY                                 3

HOLD UP. IT'S STARTING TO FEEL LIKE I     11
CAN'T SAY ANYTHING…

WHEN IT DOESN'T WORK                           19

WHEN IT WORKS                                  21

THAT'S A WRAP                                  23

# THE WAITING LINE

## WHAT TO DO (AND NOT DO) WHEN SOMEONE YOU LOVE IS STRUGGLING WITH INFERTILITY

By Meg Keys

# INTRODUCTION

You decided you wanted to have a baby? Fun! So, you have sex, wait two weeks and boom – you're on the road to Baby Town. Unless you're the unlucky 1 in 8 whose story doesn't go this smoothly.

That person decides they want to have a baby, has sex, waits two weeks and... no baby. So, they try again. And again. And on and on like this for months. Quite possibly years. You may see this person every day and not even know this is happening behind the scenes. But trust me, it's there.

Meanwhile, their friends are falling pregnant all around them. And everyone keeps asking, "When are YOU going to have a baby?"

This person is sitting through baby showers, visiting friends and their new baby in the hospital, and being inundated with baby pictures on social media. And they're thrilled to support their friends and family. Trust me. They are.

But they're desperately waiting for their turn. And it consumes their life. It's excruciating.

If you have a friend or family member who is experiencing infertility, this book is for you. You're great for wanting to help your friend and "get it right." You're great for seeking out this book. (And I'm not just saying that because I wrote it!)

It can be tough to know what to do or say to help. This book is meant to be a quick guide to help you navigate this precarious journey.

Make no mistake about it – you're likely going to get it wrong. Not because you're not a good person, but because the hormones and heartache of infertility make for an emotional landmine that's nearly impossible to navigate.

But you care and you're trying and you can do this! And this book will help. Remember, your person needs you no matter how stoic she may seem.

Let's dive in!

# WHAT NOT TO SAY

*"Would you consider adoption?"*
Don't say it. The end.

Ok, that's not the end. But for some reason this question is often where people begin. And here's the deal with it: The question of adoption carries a host of assumptions – mainly that all hope is lost, and adoption is the only choice (whether or not you mean it that way or not). Give your person credit – she knows adoption exists. She knows it's an option but she's not there right now. It's best not to go there until she does.

*"Have you tried _____!?"*
Likely, your person has tried it all. And if they haven't, it's because they don't want to, or they aren't there yet or that approach isn't their path to take.

Everyone is different, and what worked for you or someone you know doesn't mean it's what your person needs to do to make a baby.

Now if they ASK you for input or advice, go for it. But until they ask you point blank, kindly cool it on the unsolicited advice.

Plus, keep in mind that they're under the care of a doctor. So, anything they absolutely should be doing, their doctor will tell them to do.

### *"Maybe you're not doing it right..."*
We are.

People struggling to get pregnant are the queens of Googling! So yes, we've all heard of basal temperature tracking, special lubricants, we know to put our legs in the air after doing the deed (or laying on our stomach if we have a tilted uterus), we've gained weight or lost weight, used ovulation predictor kits, drank pomegranate juice, tried acupuncture, switched to decaf coffee, taken prenatal vitamins and ALL the supplements in between... we've tried it all.

Infertility isn't about someone having sex incorrectly, and unfortunately, there's no simple solution.

### *"Just relax and it'll happen!"*
There is no 'just' in infertility.

Some people have medical conditions that prevent

them for getting pregnant without medical intervention. Telling your person to "just relax" or to "just stop trying" isn't accurate or helpful.

It can also make your person feel like they're doing something wrong by going to such great lengths to have a baby, or stressing too much, or overreacting. And they're not.

### *"You're lucky you still have your freedom. Go on vacation and enjoy yourself while you can!"*
This kind of comment is well intended but your person definitely doesn't feel lucky to be in her situation. And anyway you shake it, infertility is no freedom.

Not only does it feel like your body is forsaking you every month, but infertility treatments can be extremely expensive. (There goes the vacation fund.)

Factor in the number of doctor appointments during a treatment cycle, as well as potential side-effects from all the medication, and your person is likely in no mood to go on vacation, even if she could fit it into her budget or schedule.

### *"You want to take one of my kids off my hands? I'm exhausted!"*
Yes, please.

Your person would give anything to have a child and be exhausted like you. So, while joking about taking one of your kids is meant to be cute, it stings.

And if you have twins… same thing goes. You certainly have your hands full, but jokingly asking, "Want one?" is tough to take.

### "Watch my kids for one day and I promise you won't want any of your own!"

Your person is so excited to experience parenting for herself, including all the highs and lows. In fact, she can't wait to be frustrated and pulling her hair out, just like you. I promise a few hours with your kids isn't going to take that away your person's irrepressible urge to make a baby.

### "Have you thought about doing IVF?"

Talking about IVF can feel really scary to someone going through infertility struggles. It's often viewed as a last resort, even if simply due to cost.

Asking about scary next steps creates anxiety. Just have faith things will work out for your person and let them take the lead when talking about next steps.

### "My friend's aunt's best friend's sister did IVF and got pregnant with twins!"

We know success is possible, that's why we're seeking out fertility assistance and hoping against all hope that it works. But hearing about someone else's happily ever after when we're in the midst of fighting so hard for our own, doesn't always land the way you intend.

You mean well when you tell us about success stories, and we totally get that. But every situation is different, and every person is different, so it can sometimes feel isolating to hear stories about other people's success. (Because perhaps that person didn't have PCOS, or low ovarian reserve, or endometriosis, or fibroid tumors, or whatever the case may be for your person.)

### Don't tell stories about how easily you get pregnant.

While this seems like a no-brainer... it needs to be said: When your person tells you she's having trouble getting pregnant, don't chime in with stories about how easily you seem to get pregnant and that your nickname is "Fertile Myrtle". And skip the part about how you WISH you had that problem because little Ronnie was an "Oopsie Baby".

We get that it happens easily for a lot of people. But your person isn't one of them.

### *"Have you considered using a surrogate?"*

This one is in the same family as asking about adoption.

But this one stings in its own unique way because it suggests your person can't carry a baby, which may not be the case at all. Often infertility issues arise due to egg quality issues – and a million other things – and has nothing to do with the woman's uterus.

As a general rule, until your person mentions wanting to seek out a surrogate, don't ask about it.

### Stop asking if they're pregnant yet.

You're hopeful and optimistic that you're going to hear some good news any day now. We get it!

But repeatedly asking if your person is pregnant makes her feel awkward and reminds her that she isn't pregnant... yet, again. (Or, maybe she actually IS pregnant, but waiting to share until a certain medical milestone.)

So, as a general rule, don't arbitrarily ask if your person is pregnant and just assume she isn't. When she actually is pregnant and ready to tell you, she will.

### Avoid speaking in proverbs.

You know, comments like, "If it's meant to be, it will

be," and "Everything happens for a reason," and all that jazz.

While I'm a huge fan of inspirational quotes, comments that imply your person isn't meant to have a baby can be pretty hurtful.

No one really knows why things happen. So, let's not go there.

### "At least you have one child."
Infertility after you've already had a child is called "secondary infertility" and it's more common than you may think.

Having a child doesn't take away the pain of being unable to have more. Especially if you've always imagined your future family being bigger, and dreamt of giving your child a sibling or two.

Couples experiencing secondary infertility are grateful for what they have, and also sad over what they don't have at the same time. And that's ok.

### "Whose fault is it? Yours or his?"
Even though your person confided in you that she's struggling with infertility, don't assume that she's now up for sharing all the details.

And it's certainly nobody's "fault."

Let your person take the lead on what she wants to share and not share.

# HOLD UP. IT'S STARTING TO FEEL LIKE I CAN'T SAY ANYTHING...

Here's the deal: This situation is impossible for you to know exactly what to say or do, and we get that! There is no quick fix. If anything was that easy, we would be doing it. Trust me. So, what SHOULD you say and do?

Let's jump in...

### *"Tell me everything you want to share about how it's going."*

We want to talk about it. Our lives revolve around it. It's at the center of everything we do and most of the decisions we make while in the thick of treatment, even while everything else on the surface seems normal. So, trust me when I say we want you to ask how it's going, and acknowledge it.

Ask how it's going and listen until your person is

done talking. Don't rush them to stop because you feel uncomfortable or they start crying or whatever the case may be.

Ask, and then listen, listen, listen. Say, "tell me more" from time to time. Let them know you're in no rush to change the subject until they're ready to stop talking.

## Ask questions.

Ask about your person's treatment plan and note significant test days. It means a lot to get a text from a friend on important milestone appointment days.

Questions like, "How does that work?" are totally fine, too. Don't feel like you're supposed to know it all (or anything!).

Skip the part about, "All this fertility stuff is SO scary! I can't even imagine." And, "Do you have to take shots? Eek! I could never do that. I hate shots."

We wish we weren't doing this. We hate shots, too. But we do what we have to do. Acting astonished at our struggle can feel isolating.

Bottom line: Anyone battling infertility is a badass. It takes guts and grit. Remind us of that when the going gets tough.

## Don't be silent.

Infertility is a super awkward topic (especially if you have children and can't relate) and sometimes fearing you'll say the wrong thing can make you feel like saying nothing at all. But silence can be confusing and can make your person feel bad. If your person told you about her infertility struggles, make it a point to check in.

## Here's a super simplified breakdown of the most common treatments:

- **Clomid:** This is a common approach often used as "step 1" when someone is having trouble getting pregnant. It is a pill. You either take it for a number of days and then have sex when ovulating, or it can be used in conjunction with intrauterine insemination.

- **Intrauterine Insemination (IUI):** This is where they shoot sperm directly into the uterus. Big Days: insemination days - usually one or two days. This is preceded by medication to get the woman's eggs to grow, which may be in the form of a pill or shots.

- **In Vitro Fertilization (IVF):** This is where they take the woman's eggs out of her body and fertilize them in a petri dish. This is preceded by medication to get the woman's eggs to grow. The medication is in the form of shots and often includes multiple medications and multiple shots per night. They take the eggs out via a minor surgery and then put them back in (timing on the 'put back in' varies). Big Days: egg retrieval, embryo transfer, and approximately 14 days after. In those 14 days (known as the "two-week wait"), your person is on pins and needles. Her nerves are on edge because every little symptom has her spinning down a path of "what ifs." It's absolute torture.

## About the Big Days:

At the very least, ask when these appointments are happening so you can follow up on those days by sending a text or giving her a call.

Here is a sample text that would be perfect in any of these situations:

> *"Thinking of you today! Sending positive thoughts that all goes really well! Let me know how it goes if you feel like texting back or calling. Otherwise, I'll catch up with you soon to hear all about it.*
> *XOXO"*

Keep in mind: Infertility is a tough journey that your person is battling, mostly alone. Even if she's in a relationship, the woman carries the brunt of the burden. It's the ultimate mind game and test of will. And even your strongest friend or family member could use some cheering on throughout the process.

## Send cards.

Sending a card may sound old school (and yes, it's a hassle to buy stamps) but the gesture goes a really long way.

Inside, write the following:

> *"You are a rock star! You've got this, I'm here for you, I believe in you, I think of you all the time. I'm proud of you.*
> *Love, [Your name]"*

Reminder: Skip the part about, "I can't even imagine what you're going through" and, "I don't know how you do it." She does it because she has to.

## Send random texts.

When your person is going through fertility treatments, text her to say, "Thinking of you! Cheering you on and sending hugs!"

A simple acknowledgement that this huge event is taking place in their life is important.

## Send socks.

That's right, socks! Adorable, cozy socks.

Infertility treatments involve a lot of time with your feet in stirrups at a doctor's office. Fun socks are sometimes all there is to help you feel like yourself in the midst of a really awkward situation.

Give your person the gift of socks to show them you get what they're going through. When they look down at their feet, they'll be sure to smile.

## Other fun things you could do or send:

- Give a gift with anything pineapple – notebooks, pencils, water bottles, etc. The pineapple is a symbol widely used in the Trying To Conceive Community (#ttccommunity) to celebrate the hope of new life. It is also thought to help with implantation, so anything pineapple-themed makes a good gift. (And you'll look like you're really hip and in the know, too!)
- Positive quote cards, coffee mugs, journals, fun pencils or pens, colorful pill organizers (trying to make a baby means taking a lot of supplements and pills), manicure/pedicure gift cards.
- Mantra bracelets or jewelry with positive messages.
- Send a cookie gram or fruit bouquet. This would be a fun idea to send from a

group of friends. Flowers can be cheerful but can also come across as depressing, since people tend to send flowers during sad times. (Husbands, however, should bring their wives flowers often during infertility struggles!)

- Etsy.com is full of fertility related gifts, including t-shirts, personalized gifts, and so much more. Just search "IVF" for a ton of unique and thoughtful ideas.

- Make a playlist with uplifting/inspiring songs and share it with your person. Some good songs to get you started:

> "Roar" – Katy Perry
> "Fight Song" – Rachel Platten
> "Invincible" – Kelly Clarkson
> "I Will Wait" – Mumford & Sons
> "Elastic Heart" – Sia
> "Calling All Angels" – Train
> "In the Waiting Line" – Zero 7
> "Beauty in the World" – Macy Gray
> "Have a Little Faith in Me" – Joe Cocker
> "Like a Prayer" – Madonna
> "O-o-h Child" – The Five Stairsteps
> "Rainbow" – Kacey Musgraves
> "Rise Up" – Andra Day
> "Shake it out" – Florence + the Machine
> "S.O.B." – Nathaniel Rateliff & The Night Sweats

"Take Me Home" – Phil Collins

"Lately" – David Gray

## Keep in mind:

- It's probably best to steer clear of alcohol or coffee gifts. Many women avoid these things when undergoing fertility treatments.
- Some say that keeping your body warm during treatment helps create a welcome place for baby to implant. So, if you're going to bring your person a meal, stick to soups and warm casseroles and skip the ice cream.

# WHEN IT DOESN'T WORK

After all the medication, shots, doctor appointments, money, highs, lows, ups and downs, getting a negative pregnancy test result is devastating. It's best to tread lightly but don't bow out at this point.

This would be the perfect time for Starbucks gift cards or a bottle of wine. But just leave the gift on your person's front porch and text them after you've dropped it off. They likely won't be up for visitors.

Cards with a thoughtful acknowledgement are a safe bet, but as always, be careful about what you say. A simple, "I'm thinking of you and sending big hugs" is perfect.

Skip the part about "You'll get pregnant next time," or "At least you can drink wine again," or "Now you can go on vacation and enjoy yourself," or... you get the picture.

All your person wants is to be pregnant. There are

Meg Keys

no silver linings when it doesn't work. Just keep it short and sweet and you'll be good to go.

# WHEN IT WORKS

If you know your person is closing in on the end of her two-week wait and will be testing for pregnancy soon, give her space.

Of course, some people love to share every detail of the process (including their pregnancy test results the moment they pee on a stick), but others want to deal with this extremely emotional moment in private.

While it's important to ask questions and check-in at some critical stages of her process, this is one time where laying low may be more appropriate.

Even when the test is positive, don't be surprised if your person isn't shouting the results from the mountain tops right away. And certainly, don't take it personally if they wait to tell you their good news. Because while you may think, "They're pregnant! Yay! The struggle is OVER!" your person may be thinking, "This is amazing and I'm SO happy, but I have a lot of hills to climb before I'll let myself really believe this is happening."

Those hills could include seeing a heartbeat on the ultrasound, graduating from their infertility doctor's office and moving on to their regular OB's office (a major milestone for infertility patients), making it to 12-weeks (when some risk of miscarriage declines) and much more.

When you've tried so hard to make a baby and finally achieve success, it's common to feel nervous it will go away at any moment. Especially, if you've experienced a pregnancy loss in the past.

So be excited and happy, of course! But let your person lead the way in terms of celebrating, announcing and preparing for baby. Certainly, don't post anything on social media or tell anyone just yet (not even close family members) – it's your person's story to tell.

# THAT'S A WRAP

If you find yourself thinking, "Oh no, I hope I didn't do that!" or, "Oops, did I say that?" Don't worry! Even if you said and did everything in this book I said you *shouldn't* do, you're still great. Because you're trying.

In fact, your person has a very special message for you. (Yes, *you!*)

> *"Thank you. Thank you for seeking out a book like this because you care so much. Thank you for thinking of me. Thank you for worrying about me. Thank you for having faith in me. Thank you for wanting my dreams to come true. I love you and appreciate you even when I'm so wrapped up in my infertility journey that I can't see straight. I appreciate you."*

Just remember – the fact that you're concerned about being a good friend or supportive family member is proof that you already are one.

Meg Keys

Made in the USA
Middletown, DE
05 December 2019

80045543R00018